"We are ... on
that you l ...

MW01204916

Howard Ely, Managing Editor,
The International Library of Poetry

"This poem has a strong emotional core ... with good rhythms and a strong end."

Len Roberts, Chairman,
ILP Editorial Review Board in his review of
"Fate of the Rhymer"

"Joy, I was extremely delighted with your work and feel you deserve this type of recognition. Many people write poetry for years and never obtain the level of artistry that is present in your work. You should be very proud of your accomplishment."

Nigel Hillary, Publisher, Poetry Division,
Noble House U.K.

"*Findings: My Journey to Joy* is a delightful compilation of thoughtful and challenging poetry. The author will take you on her journey and have you experiencing the emotional roller-coaster that brought her through these challenging times in her life. The author has poured her heart and soul into this book, and I know that you will enjoy her journey."

Charles E. Seevers, Director, Kids For Christ International

truly inspired by the unique talent and artistic visio
have displayed ..."

FINDINGS: MY JOURNEY TO
JOY

A COLLECTION OF POEMS

JOY S. TAYLOR

TATE PUBLISHING *& Enterprises*

 TATE PUBLISHING
& Enterprises

Tate Publishing is committed to excellence in the publishing industry. Our staff of highly trained professionals, including editors, graphic designers, and marketing personnel, work together to produce the very finest books available. The company reflects the philosophy established by the founders, based on Psalms 68:11,

"THE LORD GAVE THE WORD AND GREAT WAS THE COMPANY OF THOSE WHO PUBLISHED IT."

If you would like further information, please contact us:
1.888.361.9473 | www.tatepublishing.com
TATE PUBLISHING & Enterprises, LLC | 127 E. Trade Center Terrace
Mustang, Oklahoma 73064 USA

Findings: My Journey to Joy

Cover design by Janae Glass
Interior design by Jennifer Redden

Published in the United States of America
ISBN: 978-1-6024703-3-X
07.01.24

DEDICATION

I dedicate this project to my parents. My father is currently residing with the Lord and watching over my keyboard. I miss him profoundly, and I look forward to spending eternity talking over my growth in the Lord and how it affected my self-discovery. My mother is battling Alzheimer's disease. When I can spend time with her, we have wonderful moments together that I cherish. Even though she can't recall them too long after they fly past, I can, for the time being, remember them for both of us. I dedicate my work to my children: Robin, Matt, Jannette, Tom, and Renee. They are grown and out of the house now. Memories, sometimes happy and sometimes sad, hide in the corners of every room in my house. Now and then I pull them out and replay them. My children are a constant source of inspiration. I am grateful for their contribution to my life; they have enriched my existence and brought me great pride in who they have become as adults. I include in my dedication the circle of friends who surrounded me with their loving support, helping me clean up the mess and pick up the pieces during and after my divorce. I dedicate my book to Christ, my Savior, my strength, my greatest ally, my confidant, my source of wisdom and vision. Without His intervention and saving grace, I would have succumbed long ago to the fate of permanent invisibility. I pray my writing points my readers directly to the one true God, whose grace covers me. I dedicate this book to those readers who struggle with identity and self-worth issues as I do.

ACKNOWLEDGEMENTS

I would like to thank God for the constancy He shows me. He has written upon my heart and soul, "I love you. I accept you. I empower you. I encourage you. You are beautiful. You are mine. You are worthy. I will always love you."

TABLE OF CONTENTS

LIFE

FINDINGS: MY JOURNEY TO
JOY

A COLLECTION OF POEMS

JOY S. TAYLOR

HOPE

FOREWORD

As a child, my bedroom window overlooked a lake; and each morning, as I would get ready for my day, there would be a different scene created for me. In the spring the scene was sparkling with a drop of the sun on the water. In the summer months, the warm southern mornings shown off the refreshing dazzle of the inviting waters. The reflection of creation invited daydreaming and pure peace. In the coolness of autumn mornings the surroundings changed as the stage was set with a fresh look rippling over the water. Even in the bitterness of winter, the reflection of bare limbs promised new life. As life finds us in different seasons of life, Joy Taylor's writings can bring *hope* when life feels hopeless, *healing* when life feels broken, and *honor* when life feels strong. Joy's writing is her path to healing, as her life, like us all, has taken her through some deep winters. But as we all know, winter is trumped each year by a blooming spring. That same life is found in our Lord. As Joy has so passionately written, her hope comes from the name of the Lord, where all of our help comes from!

Michael Frost
Worship and Music Minister
First Christian Church of Florissant

PREFACE

Dear Reader,

Life is a journey. Physically, we move through time from cradle to grave. Hopefully, we learn something and grow along the way. Our path winds up peaks of elation, down valleys of tragedy, over rivers of tears. Each day we wake to face a new set of wanderings taking us closer to the end of the trail. Where we end up physically isn't important. Where we end up spiritually is everything.

I wrote the poems I've compiled here from the time just prior to my divorce to now, a few years after its finality. I learned divorce wasn't the end of life and time that I thought it would be. It was only a bend in my life's path toward a different reality, where singleness is not a monster in the dark. It is a state of wholeness in Christ.

Though I touch on a mix of topics, I've divided my work among groupings of losing and finding friends, losing and finding love, losing and finding life, and finally finding hope. I discovered that all my searching for some friend, child, or partner to rescue me was futile. No human can fill that role. When I found a bond with Christ, I found me. I found Joy. I found grace. I found solace. I found hope.

I pray my poems reflect my growth from a dysfunctional wife and mother into a fulfilled woman of God. Let me take you on my journey to Joy.

Sincerely,

Joy S. Taylor

FRIENDSHIP

A FRIEND OF MINE

Once upon a time I was a friend of mine
But somewhere in the crush of life
I lost just who and where and what I was
I gave up on the best of me
Put aside the rest of me
Replaced my identity
With mystery and fuzz
Not saving some for times to come
Left none of me to share and grow
For when I gave it all away
I didn't see there'd come a day
My heart and soul would know
No more of me

TO BE SEEN

I've learned to be invisible.
It's really very possible—
Discounted for the thoughts I've had,
Discounted for the life I've led,
Not one to be reckoned with,
Not one to be sorely missed.
I've learned to be invisible.
It's really very possible.
It keeps me from Rejection's door,
Should I aspire to reach for more;
But, now I'm in Invisible's berth,
Sometimes I really wish I weren't!

FRIENDS AGAIN

When I was young
I had a friend
Together we would ride
O'er meadows, trails, and mountainsides,
Together, side-by-side.
Then harsh words hit
That caused our split.
Together we're no more.
Friends so long
From grade school on
A shame we let it go.
Could I take back those words,
The thoughtless ones that hurt,
And see if in the end
We can be friends again?

ARE WE?

You and I really aren't okay, are we?
Much as I'd like our past to be different,
It never will be.
How do we overcome tears we've cried?
How do we move into the future
And let bygones go bye?
Help me work through this, for
Our relationship is worthy.
Let me begin by saying, "I'm sorry."

Please forgive me.

WHAT WOULD I DO WITHOUT MY FRIENDS?

What would I do without my friends?
I'm finding more and more as this life ends
That I can't thrive without my friends.
There when I needed a hand,
There when I took a stand.
We laughed, cried, walked and ran.
They've never left me with nowhere to turn.
They seem to know when my soul yearns
For the touch of one whose heart I've learned.
Caring, sharing, daring to be
Support for each other, support for me.
Without my friends where would I be?

I PRAYED

I prayed for you today
In my most sincere way.
I asked for grace
That you see God's face;
And that you be encouraged.

I lifted up your name
That blessings may rain
The warmth of God's love
To undoubtedly prove
In Christ, your heart will flourish.

I prayed for you today
Most earnestly did I pray
God grant you peace
And abundant release,
For Christ your soul will nourish.

THE COVERING

It covers me.
The crimson flow
Floods my soul
From outer skin
To the deep within.
I know the darkest
Secrets of my sin
Yet it covers me
The miracle forgiveness brings
Has changed my song
From desperate whimper
To words with wings
Of hope and promise,
Savior and kings.
The mystery salvation poses
Converts the healing flow
To a glowing robe
As brilliant white as snow;
And it covers me.
My underlying darkness
Is no more,
For God looks down
To see the Savior's
Cloak that covers me.

I Am Found

I surrender
I'm involved
I'm absolved
I succumb
I submit
I'm enfolded
I'm emboldened
I come
To your kindness
To your mercy
To your justice
To your goodness
To your love
For I find myself in you

GOD'S KID

A child of God am I
By decree from on high
No condemnation
For God's relation
A child of God am I
I am a sister of the King
No wonder that I sing
He paid my price
With His sacrifice
I'm a sister to the King
I'm a member of royalty
Value set by Christ on the tree
Yes, set forever
Lessened never
I'm a member of royalty
A precious one am I
Not hearing Satan's lie
I've found my place
Within God's grace
I know that here am I

LOVE

THE ONLY ONE

I'm lonely in your arms
When we make love
There is only you
You fall so deeply into you
There is no room for me
For you're the only one you see

YESTERDAY

The news I heard today
Makes me long for yesterday.
'Cause the news I heard today
Blows our hopes and dreams away.
Can we make it go away?
Can we take it back to yesterday?
Can we rewrite recent history?
Can we make it what it ought to be?
'Cause the news I heard today
Makes me long for yesterday.
Can we un-feel all the pain?
Can we un-cry tears like rain?
If I pretend it's not real
Will it change the way I feel?
When I see your wounded face
Will I have the strength for grace?
Can I look at you and say
I don't think of yesterday?
Wishing this hadn't happened,
Can I focus on what matters?
Can I change the words I heard?
Will that make it be less hard
To face the facts of yesterday
That brought the news I heard today?

Can we make it go away?
Can we take it back to yesterday?
'Cause the news I heard today
Changes everything.
It changes everything.
No, we can't go back and fix the past.
To deal with present sorrows,
We have only our tomorrows;
And what shall we do with these, my love?
What shall we do with these?

THE PROBLEM

You know, I have a problem with you.
It's not what you say. It's what you do.
You say you love me, I don't think it's true.
And that's why I've a problem with you.
The stars count the memories of brighter days
But the morning tears fade them all to gray.
I found a note sincere and heartfelt
Not meant for me, but someone else,
Professing your love—her heart to melt
And that is the problem you have dealt.
The stars count the memories of brighter days
But the morning tears fade them all to gray.
I see trouble coming, coming our way
Not in the future, it's coming today.
You say you love me. You don't act that way.
And that's why I'm leaving, going away.
The stars count the memories of brighter days
But the morning tears fade them all to gray.
You know, I have a problem with you.
It's not what you say. Your words aren't true.
You say you're sorry, sorry won't do.
That's why we're over. I'm through with you.
The stars count the memories of brighter days
But the morning tears fade them all to gray.
Fade them all to gray.

RATHER BE RAKING

What'd your mate rather do than be with you?
Your relationship's quaking,
If they'd rather be raking.
Be watchful of drifting again and again.
A closer look need be taken,
If they'd rather be rakin'.
Are you kind and praising or harsh, razing?
Count the risk that you're taking,
If they'd rather be raking.
Accepting friendship, spiritual relationship—
In these be partaking.

Curb the urge,
No, the need to be raking.
Silence masks hurt; indifference hides aching.
Find the cure. Something's missing for sure,
If she'd rather be raking.
Don't regret it—fill the need—do you get it?
Check affection, feelings under protection?
Find out fast, cause his loving won't last,
If he'd rather be raking.

THE UNDOING

Soul in desperation,
Hoping life won't last.
What can you do now
To undo your past?

Years of angry banter
Wrought sorrowed hearts.
What can you do now
To rewrite those parts?

Do you not see?
Can you not know?
What can you do now
To unsew what's sewn?

Ask forgiveness.
Hope for grace,
Honest heart a must
To rebuild broken trust.

EYE OF THE STORM

A storm is raging; anger swells
Hearts are wounded, relived hells
Multiple storm fronts through the years
Leave hurts behind not healed by tears

New wind blowing to love's shore
This one different than before.
Waves of passion stirred to fury
Bring a harsh, rash, flashing flurry

End of the fray, enter love's hearse
Waters calmed by true remorse
Glassy surface behind the roaring
This the calm eye of the storm

Indifferent silence that won't end
Empty hearts this time don't mend
Realize the new gale form
Comes the backside of the storm

Reverse winds of separation blow
Hearts re-torn a fresh rift know
Of living life now newly born
A chance for peace beyond the storm

LIVE AND LEARN

Estranged is such a curious word.
One I'd never understood
Though I'd heard it before.
I guess it's true, you don't get it
Until you've lived it.

We started out enchanted.
Then settled for encheated.
We fell into a mode of war
Where harshness was inflicted.
We lived out lives conflicted;
And love ensued no more.

Emotions were estrained.
So I moved out, you moved on.
We became estranged
Where nothing was the same.
Dreams were lost, by torrents tossed
Strewn about to be picked up.
The pieces fit no more.

Out of sorts, out of place
Still, there was a world to face.
Should I keep my children's name?
Must I get out of bed today?
I was changed forevermore.

We tramped up the legal steps,
Dragging our baggage along.
This to you, that to me.
What was yours and mine all
Neatly packaged. Divorce is final.
We are estranged no more.

SOME DAYS

Some days are better than others.
The memories subside.
Some days are clearer than others.
No fog clouds my mind.
Some smiles come easier than others.
Now and then healing breaks through.
Now and then I don't think of you.

Some hearts know love more than others.
Yours, I doubt, is one.
Some loves last longer than others.
Ours was doomed from the start.
Some futures are brighter than others.
Mine needs a flicker of hope.
Mine is a future alone.

Some days flow better than others.
The past doesn't stalk.
Some days I grow more than others.
It's a difficult walk.
Sometimes I think I won't make it.
Lately, I know that I can.
Lately, I know that I will.

FOREVER LOVE

I once had a forever love,
At least that's what I thought
When it began so many years ago.
What started so pure and
Open and sweet and warm
Died helpless, scarred,
Nowhere left to go.
Protected, love was not.
In crept killers unhindered.
They sliced and chipped and ate away.
The trust we held,
No longer stood.
The ravage took over.
We let the killers hold sway.

It all seemed in fun—
A joke gone awry.
Sarcasm, criticism part of the game.
But the fun turned sour
When hour upon hour
Conflict became our one claim to fame.
Bruised and battered,
Emotionally scattered,

We turned away from each other.
We made love a sham,
We battled 'til the one great hurt—
One from which we could not recover.
Now to forever, our love is only
A wisp of the past,
Something to long for, a dream denied.
Our hope for the future,
If given the chance,
To protect a new love proven and tried.

THE COLORS OF LOVE

I've known black love,
Based on self-seeking vanity.
Crushing, usury, fake love
Drove me to the brink of insanity
And seared my soul.
I've known gray love,
A fading bad memory.
Leaving the black love.
Mourning what wouldn't be
And nursing the blow.
I've known blue love,
The true-blue of family.
Behind-the-scenes love,
Helplessly watching me
And praying for hope.
I know complete love—
Forgiving, saving, golden,
Resurrecting-my-soul love,
Touching the wound
And sealing the hole,
Chasing out darkness,
Making me whole.
I know vibrant love—

The color of sunrise:
Warm, soft, reaching-out love.
I look to each new day,
Knowing it is enough.

YOU TOUCHED ME

I'm blessed you came into my life.
God's plan—divine Providence,
Whatever the reason,
You showed up.
I cherish this season
Of friendship and faithfulness
Putting a spring in my stride.

I'm so glad you're here for me now,
Providing exactly what I need
Before I know I need it.
You've touched me.
I'm dying to repeat it,
Touched me in a way that frees me
To embrace life empowered.

I'm honored by your friendship most.
The times I struggled to survive
Whatever the reason
You showed up.
A lifeline you'd have thrown,
But a Godly step to keep me alive:
You provided a boat.

May I Touch You?

What's the point of living
If there's no one you can touch?
Everyone can use someone
Who cares that much.
Life's not supposed to be
Lived all alone.
So find one in reach
Within your touching zone,
Someone to help, someone to love
Someone to give all you have
To make their life better
And give purpose to your own.

What is It about You?

What is it about you
That has me intrigued?
I've tried to ignore you
But cannot succeed.
Your looks entice me.
Your spirit revives mine.
Your laugh sets my heart free.
Your presence divine.
Your touch sparks a fire
I cannot control.
Try, though I might,
I can't let you go.
I've worked through
My need for you.

And

I have to concede to
The fact that I love you.

WITHOUT YOU

Without you there is no song to sing
Without you there is no dream to dream
Without you there is no—
Line to rhyme
Hope for time
Air to breathe
Purpose to live
Without you there is nothing.

With you there is life.

WOULD YOU?

Would you come, come walk with me
Along life's convoluted shore,
In and out waves of trials—
Tired footsteps not tread before?

Would you come, let me love you
To my fullest, freely given,
No control to mar the beauty
No demands to make me driven?
Would you come, come walk with me
From the chapel to the grave?

Would you come, come walk with me
Through youth, midyears, and age?
Hold my hand during birth,
Cherishing my worth.
Should I change, image fade,
Can you ever be so brave?

With a cane or a walker,
Can we still go on together?
If I die first, will you manage?
Should death warrant you to stay,
Would you take the last walk with me
From the chapel to the grave?

To Dance at Your Wedding

You danced into my life
With the tiniest of toes
And the world's cutest nose.
Now you're becoming somebody's wife.

You danced onto the stage
In sequins and lace
Sporting your most angelic face.
Before I knew it, you'd come of age.

You raced through school dreams
A magnificent dance
To a military cadence.
You answered the call to honor, duty.

Today you will marry
The dance of your choice
While we all rejoice
In one unified voice.

Today it's my turn to dance.
At your wedding I'll prance
In the glow of your countenance
By the warmth of your radiance.

I have waited for this day
Your grand day of all days.
For your future I pray
From the depth of my heart:

A prayer for spiritual unity
A prayer for marital sanctity
A prayer for family harmony
A prayer for lifelong serenity
And devotion.

I LOVE YOU

I must go to work.
It's something I do
To muddle through.
I keep up the struggle
To keep things afloat.
Before I go,
I want you to know

That I love you.
You're off, too,
To do what you do
That keeps your life
Moving from day-to-day.
Before you go,
You simply must know
That I love you.

One day for sure,
My time will be through.
My life will be spent
Doing my best so
You will know
How much I've loved you.

MAKE LOVE TO ME

I'm a woman. Make love to me.
I'm on fire, but not for your body.
Your heart and soul are my desire.
Open the eyes of my heart with your care.
Brush my senses with your very being.
I'm a woman, a responder
It's not about the physical thing.
Make love to my emotions the whole day through.
I'm a woman. I know nurture.
I know how it feels to be loved,
I know how it feels to be used:
The tone of your voice,
The look in your eye,
The warmth of your touch,
The truth of your prayers,
Your openness and trust.
I'm a woman, a responder.
Help my love grow stronger.
Day by day, each day we start fresh.
Soul to soul we become one flesh.

LIFE

THE YEARS

It's autumn again and the years fall from me
Like leaves from the trees outside my door.
Oh, I'm not so very old, yet—
Old enough to have stories to tell
And some to regret.
The years roll by, they just roll by.
You've all flown the coup, reached high
Toward your goals. It's just ... sometimes
I miss the signs you and I were young.
You backing up to sit on my knee
Squeals from water fights, balls in the yard
Hair bands galore, yet none to be found.
The years roll by, they just roll by.
Now the yard waits for someone to come play
And no one seeks the hair bands that got away.

A PERSON OF COLOR

I am a person of color.
When you consider it,
Really now, who isn't?
My color is white,
Decorated with speckles
Of age spots and freckles.
Truth be told,
May I be so bold
As to be a holder
Of multiple colors?

SUNSET FROM ABOVE

Yesterday, I saw God's Gates of Heaven open
Over a graveyard with the sun's rays
Reaching to the headstones in the turf.
I saw them kiss the earth.
Today, I had a thrill during my flight home.
For the first time, I saw sunset from above the clouds.
The sun's rays lit the layers from the bottom up.
They streaked from their source at the horizon,
Up through the heavens to the plane I was in.
I watched the sky beneath me blush,
Lightly at first, then darker in acknowledgement
Of God's loving touch.

Life's Path

I walk through life on a path
Of my own choosing.
Through a wide expanse
of experience winds
The way of my calling—
The cobblestones treading.
Uphill climbs, down hills
Falling into the future
Of unknown plodding.
Fields of memories line the way,
Shining and brightening the day
As far as I can see.
When did it start that
My vision is dimming—
My field of vision slimming
And slimming?
Memories fall off in landslides of age.
Years pile on while faculties fade.
I'm not in control.
I have little choice.
Age will win and silence
My voice. I speak while I can.
I have to walk on

Along the path to the precipice edge
Where I write no more and
Fall over the ledge
Into the arms of my waiting Lord.

FATE OF THE RHYMER

Alzheimer's, fate of the rhymer,
Who's known the relation
For two generations.
Mother's mother, mother, daughter,
Fight the battle now and hereafter.
Medical miracles we can't see,
Only diagnoses of what is to be.
Streaming, screaming, tears we cry
Throughout this very long good-bye.
Strength of soul,
Overcome fragile mind.
Carry us through the ravage of time.
The day sure to be
When Mom will forget me.
God, help me through
The day I forget you, Mom.

HAVE YOU SEEN MY HUSBAND?

Have you seen my husband?
I just don't understand.
I guess I must have lost him,
But once I had a man.
For six decades I loved him.
Have you seen my husband?
I know his name is John.
They tell me he is gone.
He died June 1999.
I guess I must have missed it.
Have you seen my husband?
How could he disappear?
His picture is on my TV.
I'd hoped that he was here.
I just don't understand.
Have you seen my husband?
My brain's not what it was.
They tell me a disease has
Turned it all to fuzz.
I know he was a good man.
If you see my husband,
Please, tell him that I miss him.

NOW IS ALL WE KNOW

Not now, I'll cry later, after the
Long good-bye ends.
I'll have time to let down then.
You're with me now, this instant, this minute,
This second is all you know.
A year or two ago, you knew me.
Today, as another, you construe me.
Yet, I know you know who I am, who I was.
The youngest daughter of all you bore.
Tomorrow, perhaps, you'll know me no more.
This moment we share, our eyes and souls meet.
I'll remember, though you can't.
I'll carry the memory for you and for me.
Today is the day; it's all we have.
Now is the hour that passes too fast.
This is the moment, this one we share.
This one, this very one is all I care to cherish.
The next one is new, and you may not know me.

MADELYN

Madelyn, sweet Madelyn
So beautiful and feminine
Tiny nose, tiny toes you have
With ears just like your dad
I'm thrilled I got to hold you
I'm happy to have told you
How much you're loved
By God above
Your tiny cheek I kissed
How sorely you are missed.

Rise Up

Up, rise up
Through the gray mist of mid-day fog
To the sun.
Up, rise up
Never fearing what may come
Or has gone.
Fly, oh, fly.
Leave the dreary gloom of heavy
Loads carried.
Soar, yes, soar
To the sun-drenched side
Of the clouds
Far, far above
The ocean of life's cares.
Up, rise up.
When you come to your end,
Rise up!

FLY TO THE LIGHT

Carry me,
Bright star of Jesus,
To the horizon,
Over to Zion.
Move to the Hope.
Draw me on,
Winged feet of the Master,
To the One calling,
To the One calling.
Run to I Am.
Pull me close,
Precious arms of the Father,
Until forever,
Loose me never.

JOEY

Shadows of you
Are all that are left.
A glint of a memory
A voice from the past
Swirls in my head as
Part of my dreams.
It wakes me from sleep.
"Joey," it calls, "Joey."
It falls on the ears of my heart,
And I miss you.
Nobody used my name in that way;
None before you and nobody since.
"Joey." I hear it clearly,
Just like when you were
Here with me, fixing the car,
Tending the pets.
"Joey." How can it be
That you call to me, "Joey?"
Because you are gone,
I have to move on.
I can't touch you.
I can't reach you.
I loved the way
You called me, "Joey."

KATIE DID

Who knew me well before
I knew myself?
Who rocked and cradled me,
Putting sleep on the shelf?
        Katie did.
Who kissed my booboo's and
Daubed my boohoos?
Who chased away fears of
Snakes and voodoos?
        Katie did.
Who pushed me, pulled me,
Loved me, schooled me?
Who nurtured, molded,
And then released me?
        Katie did.
Who wished me the best and
Missed me longest?
Who prayed for me through life's
Gales strongest?
        Katie did.

RACHEL

Miss Rachel, winsome eyes of blue,
This is me, how do you do?
Tender life so full of Spirit
I wonder, how is it
I'm so blessed to watch
You learn and grow
Kindergarten graduation
Puzzles solved, pianos played
Soccer games and dragons slain
Twinkle little princess maid
Rollerblading in the heat
I just can't wait to see
What it is life has in store for
Miss Rachel, queen of all you know
Ruler of your destiny
Guided by infinitely more
Love than you may realize:
Apple of your Father's eyes.

A Prayer for Jon

Jonathan Taylor means
"Yahweh has given."
Jon—parent distracter
The mighty X-Factor
God's gift from Heaven
Determined and driven

In you I see virtues,
Though disguised by youth
Strength of will growing
Love of God showing
Independent, aloof
Your future is proof

That indeed you are
One of God's chosen few
Able to stand
A talented man
Proving your worth,
Sharing God's Truth

May God walk with
You in Wisdom's favor,
Guide your way
Hear you pray
Leading you ever
As God's kid forever

Miss O

Olivia Kate,
What do you make
Of the fate
That you face?

Too little now
To understand how
Life will allow
You to grow.

My little dear,
Nothing to fear
In the years
Coming clear.

As you strive to
Master your drive to
Be more than alive,
Heartily thrive!

ORRIN, SUPERHERO

Hodge-podge master dodge
Who are you this morning?
Is it Superman today
Or Rescue Hero play?
Riding on the rains,
Leaping through the flames,
Changing to the Hulk, then
Jumping from your bunk.
Learning from reality
These heroes are a fantasy.
The only heroes that you need
Are Mom and Dad and Jesus.
Like Jesus' sacrifice,
Mom and Dad pay a price.
Oh, you are a worthy lad
To have a Mom and Dad
Who love you more than life
And guide you in what's right.
You're their superhero
All you need to be is you.

ROYAL NAME

Nolan Earl Graham
You have three names
Before your last.
I love the way it
Rolls off my tongue
When I say it.
Nolan Earl Graham
So smooth, but manly,
Stately and grand.
You do it honor, Nolie,
My man, it serves you well.
A name to take you far,
It lets us know just who you are.

CHINA DOLL

Silken curls a-fly
Crystal eyes a-flame
Shoe toes scuffed with fun
Fragile looks belie
Waves of boundless energy
Screams announce desire
Ever on the run
Unleashed curiosity
Olivia divine
Porcelain come alive
Olivia Susanne
Sprightly heir of mine
Long may you flourish
High may you rise
Reach for your dreams
Show me your courage

FIND YOUR WAY

Where are you going, young man?
How will you fend?
Do you know where your journey ends
Before you begin?
See your way far down the road
As far as you can see.
Look into your future to be
Ready come what may.
Know the prize for which you strive.
Pray, God will lead.
You are His. He is yours.
He will hear your plea.
You're God's kid, yes, His son.
As with Jesus, you are one
With Yahweh, Almighty,
Ruler of eternity
With whom all things are possible.
Your dreams, your hopes, and goals
Your strength comes from the greatest love
This world has ever known.
He sacrificed His son for you.
Now, you do the same
To do your best, give all you have

To glorify His name.
We have one purpose in this life
So go and do your thing.
With every choice you make, my friend
Just glorify the King.
I have perfect faith in you
To rise above the crowd.
No doubt your greatest efforts, son
Will make your Father proud.

LETTING GO

You're here with me, but for how long?
Today a constant presence,
Tomorrow you are gone.
I love you, raise you, scolding, praising.
Then, off you go to take your wings.
It's part of life and nothing wrong.
Who have I after you leave us?
Don't despair, go on, succeed.
I have myself, and I have Jesus.

You're the arrow from my quiver
Launched into a troubled world.
Be a true and honest liver
Always leaning on God's Word.
So go now, raise the banner
God is asking you to carry
In your life's work and the manner
That you love. Don't tarry.
Get it on.

YOUR PLAN

Clouds of history, disguising destiny,
Get in the way of what I would be.
Son, please, come shine on me.
Blank out my yesterday.
Burn the fog away.
Let me see the
Purpose
You have for me.
Dispel the darkness,
My shadows and fears.
Let me know you are here,
Guiding my days. Leading my way
To fulfill your plan for me for all eternity.

To Leave a Mark

Another famous person passed today
Part of the story of my days
As he was in many ways
Woven through millions of lives
He goes down in history's scene
What of us this side of the screen?
What is it that we bring
To make a mark on time?
History's pages turning, turning,
Just keep turning
Life's candle burning, burning
'Til the wick runs out
Nothing to do to stop the turning
We dare not snuff out the burning
Nothing left for you and me
But to turn up our flames' intensity
And scorch a page of history
This day, before it turns
Etch my name in someone's mind
A random act, thoughtful, kind
Little hope of reaching millions
But I start
And heart-by-heart
Will leave my mark

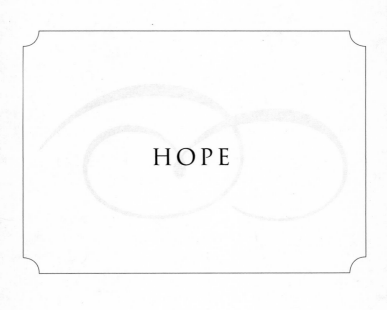

HOPE

FINGERPRINTS OF GOD

You're the hand of God, you know.
You are the hand of God.
You reached into my life today.
You lit up the path I trod.
I look into your eyes, you show
The very heart of God.

One hand holds fast to His great Truth,
The other reaches for the lost,
The sick, the hurting loved by God,
Though shaken now and tempest tossed.
Reach through the fury. Be the proof.
You are the hand of God.

You're the touch of God, you know.
You are the touch of God:
Almighty presence hard to fathom
Reality from Spirit's prod.
Make known His love wherever you go:
The fingerprints of God.

FOREVER GIFT

Motherhood, gift of life
Full of wonder, tinged with strife
Fraught with heartache, worth the struggle
Sent from heaven, God's sweet bundle

Life's a gift, yes that is true
Passed down to generations new
Gift of flesh and blood and soul
Yet something more to make me whole

Sharing faith, Mom guided me
Times of stress she prayed for me
Till I reached my own heart's route
Through Christ our Lord to the God of Truth.

Shining Glory, saving Grace
Reflected in my mother's face
Life on earth, her gift now mine
Life with God, that spans all time

Forever gift opened the door
To know God's Grace forever more.
Power of prayer; might of her faith
Wrought salvation of this lost waif

Echo Divine

The echo divine
To melt hearts such as mine:
"I love you," "I forgive you,"
Oh, to show grace such as Thine.

The habit is mine
To give as I get.
There's an echo in life
Not quite fathomed as yet
"Curse you," I shout
To those I chew out.
"Curse you," bounces back,
Undiminished by lag.
"Bless you," I whisper
To whomever I mentor.
"Bless you back," I hear,
Though not very clear.

Were it reversed
I would truly prefer
"Bless you," to shout
And "Bless you," return.
But life is a mix,

A most terrible fix,
For "Curse yous" are risen,
Though "Bless yous" are given.

Christ's example we have
To return good for bad
The echo divine
For souls such as mine.

TRIUNE

Father, Son, and Holy Spirit
Three in One I do believe
All in one and one in all
Without all three there's nothing to it

So with the life of Christ, my Lord
Birth, to death, to life anew
All three for one required belief
As stated in His Holy Word

Christmas signs forever hope
Crucifixion the promise fulfilled
Resurrection for my redemption
The three together with life to cope

Now God sees me as he sees Jesus
Cloaked in purity, justified
Mystery of mysteries
Christ gave His worth from sin to free us.

ABOUT ME

Christmas meaning left behind
Obscured by tinsel,
Twinkle lights, gifts received,
Raucous nights of merriment,
Drink and food
Running store-to-store,
Door-to-door
To see what's there for me
The biggest package 'neath the tree
With glitzy bow and wrapping bright
Is that one meant for me?
The manger calls and
My heart falls. I forget
It's not about me.
I forget it's not really about me.

THE TREE

My eyes drift up
Along a sandstone pillar
Fingers of cold stone
Reaching for the sky
Stretching to heaven
At the top grows a cedar
Out of context, out of place
No soil to nurture
No water to sustain
Yet it flourishes
Strong and stoic
Rooted in a crack
Fifty feet high
Started by a tiny seed
Lifted by the breath of God
Placed in harsh conditions
To make it or die
Trusting in its creator
Supplier of needs
Sustainer of the universe
Stoop to hear my plea
El Shaddai—the Mighty One
Giver of eternity
Sustainer of my soul
Grow me in this
Stone-cold world

CARE FOR A SOUL

Master, you urge me, care for a soul.
How can I do that? I'm hardly whole.
How do I heal someone's heart wounds, deep?
Where do I turn, my brother to keep?
Master, you tell me, pray for your brothers.
But my wounds come first,
        before those of others.
My needs are great, you know me full well.
Put them aside when others need help?
Master, you guide me, "Child, don't you know?
Turn first to Me, your strength will grow.
I am sufficient, my Word says it clear.
You can do all things through Christ without fear."
Master, I praise you, you never fail me.
Help me, guide me, help me press on.
Mend my life and make me whole.
You are the One who cares for my soul.

THIS DAY

This day in heaven will you be with me,
Where the angels sing and souls are free.
This day in heaven will you long no more
To commune with loved ones gone on before.
This day in heaven your sins are gone
Farther from you than the setting sun.
Don't think you aren't worthy of pardon's relief.
This day for heaven you need only believe.
So spoke Jesus from his cross to the thief.
So speaks Jesus to you and to me.

A Little Bit of Heaven

Jesus came to earth and was crucified.
His life for our sin was the price he paid.
The Light of the Spirit left in His stead:
A little bit of heaven for our lives.

Acceptance of Christ; the Spirit comes in.
We're then to share this gift we've taken
A little bit of heaven in souls to awaken
To light the way and to shine within.

The Spirit's the way, His love shines through.
I see when you smile, I surmise,
A little bit of heaven in your eyes.
The Spirit in me sees the Spirit in you.

Bring your little bit of heaven in any case.
A little bit of heaven here on earth,
A little bit of heaven; the soul's true worth.
We'll share a little bit of heaven in this place.

BLESSINGS

Drip, drip, drip on me,
Your blessings fall like rain
One tiny drop, then another
Again and yet again
A blessing droplet gathers
Drip, drip, drip on me
So many I can't count them
How can I catalogue them
How can I pay them back
Drip, drip, drip on me
Blessings keep on coming
Dawn to dusk, dusk to dawn
The hidden treasure is
I get to pass them on.

CALL TO WORSHIP

The pews fill with souls.
Faces blank and pale, emotionless,
Unsmiling, bodies motionless,
Eyes without sparkle all face forward,
Searching for hope. Stressed to
Our limit, we hold on in fear.

We gaze at the cross—draped in white,
Void of a body, bathed in light.
Do we know or understand?
Our hope lies in its emptiness.
The body is gone, yet God is near
For Jesus is here.

Come, worship with me; lift up a song
That moves you and awakens joy,
Overshadowing fear, stress, and emptiness.
Open your heart to your neighbor.
Share worship together.
Find hope In God's house.

Let the light of His love shine from your eyes.
Smile while you sing that Jesus is King.
Come worship with me for you are
My brother, my sister.
I'm glad that you came
On this Glorious day!

GENEALOGY OF HOPE

Love begat forgiveness.
Forgiveness begat hope.
Hope begat promise.
Promise begat the Son.
The Son revealed schism.
Schism begat hate.
Hate crucified the Son.
The Son requested forgiveness.
Forgiveness begat hope, eternal.

INTERCESSION

Holy Spirit, pray for me.
Lead me to the throne of God.
Jesus, intercede for me.
Pluck me from this path I walk.
Mercy, meet my every need.
Father, hold me in your arms.
Rest my head upon your knee—
Safe from arrows, safe from harm.
Touch my heart and make me whole.
Brush my brow. Your gentle hand
Makes me know that I am yours.
In your presence I would stand.
Mighty Ruler, King of Kings,
Sacrificed Savior Divine,
Grace Giver, Spirit Lover,
Healer, Redeemer of mine,
Overseer of my soul.
Open places in my heart
Into which I dare not go.
Lift my face, your grace impart.

WALK WITH ME

Walk with me in the desert within
Where only you can
Restore my faith
And free me again.
Allure me in the dry, desperate
Longing of my soul's constriction.
For only you supply living water
To quench my burning.
Take my hand.
Walk with me.
Touch my life with
Your love everlasting.
Love that reaches to
The darkness pervading.
Love casting out loneliness
That roils around me.
Come, be my fortress.
Break down the wall built
'Round my tenderness.
Captivate my heart.
Substitute endless rest,
Endless peace,
Endless love.

FULL CIRCLE

Circles and cycles of joy and pain
Come full circle to visit again
On balance, off balance, up and down
Twisting, turning round and round
My head spinning for what to do about
Smoke rings of uncertainty, clouds of self-doubt
'Til Christ came with a lifeline:
The golden rope of eternal hope
A guide through good times and sorrow
From here to forever straight as an arrow
Never ending, never bending
Direct to the heart of God
Who shows me the way to go
Lit by the glow of His loving
Being that inspires me to keep moving
Within the circle of His Will
He wreathed my neck with His saving arms
Lifting my face to be warmed by His glory
My once-feeble, flickering flame replaced
By God's life-light garland in Jesus' name
Wrapped tightly now around my heart and soul
I'm assured of forever and forever made whole
Never again will I seek man's approval

Only to be tossed and torn by fickle removal
Of my heart's desire
Always remembering my soul's awakening
To God's own beckoning me to come
Latch onto the golden rope
I hold fast to His hope along my journey
Of *lasting* joy—into eternity